What Som
Secrets of Successful Actors
and Sue Porter Henderson,
The *Working* Actor's Friend

*"Any actor would benefit from Sue's vast
working knowledge of the theater, television and film indus-
tries. I know this personally because I have."*
Bruce Hawkins, *Working* Actor, Co-author
The Black State of the Arts:
Show Business Career Guide for African Americans

*"Tremendous time, energy and money saver. This book
and a meeting with Sue will save you immeasurably from
pursuing dead-ends and blind alleys."*
Francene Morris, *Working* Actor, Media Personality,
Radio/TV Talk Show Host
KISS-FM and PBS-TV Charlotte, N.C.

*"Sue's materials are based on the actual experiences
of those of us who have been there and done that.
If you want to be there and do that, don't miss this book!"*
Lydia Schmitt, *Working* Actor for over 20 years
Mirror Has Two Faces

*"Sue captures the nuances unknown to most actors. She
steers you in the right direction. She has been a blessing to
my career. Thanks Sue for getting me started in New York."*
Ted Sutton, *Working* Actor for over 15 years
CNN, Crossfire, featured in GI Jane and Species 2

"Whether just starting out or trying to do more principal work, this book is for you!"
Kay Gaffney, *Working* Actor
Meet Joe Black

"Sue has helped make my transition to New York smooth and successful. It's great to know that someone genuinely cares."
Gutherie Birchfield, *Working* Actor

"Thank you for trusting me Sue. You are a rare gem in the business today."
Tom Hutton, *Working* Actor

"Sue got me going in the business and still motivates me when I need it. She truly is the working actor's friend."
Charles Mazzio, *Working* Actor

"There's nobody more caring and sharing than Sue. Her book is a gold mine of both."
Lawrence Parke, Editor/Publisher
Acting World Books

SECRETS OF SUCCESSFUL ACTORS

SECRETS OF SUCCESSFUL ACTORS

Tips For Getting Acting Jobs

SUE PORTER HENDERSON

Foreword by Susan Phelps, Ph.D.

An HEI Publication
Henderson Enterprises, Inc.
New York

Henderson Enterprises, Inc.
360 East 65th Street
Suite 15-E
New York, NY 10021-6712
Tel: (212) 472-2292
Fax: (212) 472-5999
http://www.hendersonenterprises.com

Henderson, Sue Porter
Secrets of successful actors: tips for getting acting jobs
/ Sue Porter Henderson
p. cm.
ISBN 0-9667468-0-5
1. Acting-vocational guidance

The sponsoring editors for this book were
Sue Porter Henderson and John E. Stephens.
Design and production supervised by Jason Hee.
Editorial advice and marketing consultation provided
by Ashton Productions, Inc.

First Edition
First Printing January 1999
Second Printing May 1999

To the late
Albert and Louise Porter
My parents
My inspiration
The best of the best

Contents

IV. View

V. Resources For Actors

Acknowledgments

My work as a career consultant to actors gives me a powerful sense of contribution and purpose. I have been blessed and am grateful to have so many wonderful people in my life. I continue to be amazed when others arrive in my life at just the right point to urge me ever onward and upward.

This book and the ideas that fill its pages would not be possible without the care, guidance, insight and support of many wonderful people. The following are those to whom I wish to express my sincere appreciation for their special assistance and contributions to this project. I thank:

John E. Stephens, sponsoring editor for this project, my life partner and husband for keeping my spirits up throughout this process, for his unique style of motivating me with humor and patience and for being there.

Jason Hee, professional associate, designer and friend for making himself available at all hours to see this project through to completion, his ability to generate so many ideas while working under pressure and his easy going style.

Lawrence Parke, for his wisdom and encouragement. As author of several nationally known books for actors, editor of *The Agencies,* leading career builder in Hollywood and New York, my mentor and friend, Larry, a very special thank you. You have taught me so much.

Susan Phelps, Ph.D. (The Stainless Steel Magnolia™), inspirational humorist, author, media personality, professional colleague and special friend — how does one thank you for believing in me and this book, inspiring me to go the next level and for saying yes? Thank you so much for your enlightened contribution.

J. Terryl (T. Bubba) Bechtol, CSP, humorist, author and professional speaker for his contribution of motivational insights and special material for use in this book.

Deborah (Corey) Corbin, owner of Actor Mail Mailing Services, professional colleague and friend for her support, kindness and quick turnaround on preparing the materials that would launch this project.

My sister **Sally**, nephew **Brad,** and stepson **Chris** for your ongoing support and love, and **Doug Henderson** for your special contribution.

Thank you **David Cleaver** for sharing your vast knowledge of theatrical books that are of importance to actors.

In her memory, I thank **Wilhelmina Cooper**, agent, cover girl and supermodel who showed me early on that even the most successful people can find time to advise and guide those of us just starting out. She found time for me twenty-five years ago. I view her kind gesture as the legacy she left for me to emulate.

A very special thank you to those theatrical bookstores that have been with us since the beginning: The Drama Book

Shop, Inc., Samuel French, Inc., New York, Applause Theatre Books, Inc., Coliseum Books, Inc., New York and Bakers Plays, Inc., Boston.

Finally, I thank my personal friends for their support, and those industry friends and actors, personal managers, casting directors, coaches, teachers, directors, agents, professional peers and colleagues who helped me become and remain a successful actor, a *working* actor. What I learned from my experiences working with and for them over the years make this book possible. What they taught me is my book.

*"If you love acting and seek success as an actor,
Sue Porter Henderson will tell you
how to work it and work at it."*
The Stainless Steel Magnolia™

Foreword

In *Secrets of Successful Actors*, Sue Porter Henderson shows you how to be successful in the acting profession by telling you how to find work as an actor. Her book offers hundreds of valuable tips, ideas and resources for actors no matter where they may be in their professional development.

Sue knows what she is talking about because she is a successful actor and career consultant with over twenty-five years experience. As a consultant, she has helped hundreds of actors work by getting them focused on the business side of acting.

In this book Sue reveals her knowledge and expertise acquired over the years from working in the trenches as an actor. She also shares the solutions she and her colleagues developed to make their ways in the acting profession.

Sue Porter Henderson has managed a rare feat by creating a book of information that is as inspiring and motivating as it is sensible and useful—facts laced with humor, hope springs eternal from the practical detail. Her presentation is firm and focused when explaining what is required to get acting work. It is also thoughtful and reflective of her personal knowledge of the life of an actor.

If what you know is a function of how, what, where and from whom you learn it, this book is of particular value to actors because it is also unique in its perspective. Most "how-to" books about getting work as an actor are written from the vantages of those on the hiring or casting side of the business. Many others are written from the view of the acting teacher.

Henderson's *Secrets* differs from these other how-to books about the acting business because it is written for actors by actors who are still actively earning a living from acting. The information contained in this book is current and practiced daily by its author and her fellow *working* actors. It is written by one who is insightful about the organizational cultures of many casting offices as well as understanding of the personality quirks of some individual casting personnel.

Sue Porter Henderson believes that actors who want to work as actors must adopt a business-like approach. They need to be savvy, informed and current on who is who and what is what. They must be consistent and persistent in their pursuit of the work.

I know that the suggestions put forth in this book work. I know this because I used many of them when I was an actor and can attribute my acting successes to having done so.

In fact, within three months of my arrival in New York City twenty years ago, with regional theater and choral programs as my main credits, I had my first appearance on a soap opera. For the next four years I worked steadily in the entertainment business as actor, singer, dancer and standup comic. Most importantly, I made my living doing what I wanted to be doing during that period of my life.

I did not wait to work, nor did I hope to be discovered. I took personal responsibility for my life and career. I discovered myself. I chose to be successful. These are just three of the many valuable lessons Sue Porter Henderson offers you.

Sue knows that no learning is ever wasted. She knows that success breeds success. She shows you that success is a habit and skill that can be acquired, you get to decide. If you so choose, success will follow you wherever you go on your life's journey.

She knows that not everyone who is attracted to the acting profession should be an actor. But recognizes that sometimes the only way to find that out is to actually try it. She believes that even if acting turns out not to be the right career for you, you will develop skills that will serve you in any profession you may practice in the future.

Once you embrace her ideas, a meeting with Sue can take you to your next level. She is a nice person and a tough cookie. She always encourages you to do the right thing. She can show you how to "be all that you can be" and you won't have to join the Army!

While I no longer count acting among my primary occupations, I am proud of what I accomplished then and pleased at how those accomplishments still serve me now. Today I am a published author, professional speaker, inspirational humorist and media personality. I have my retirement in the bank and share my life with a fellow seeker. I believe myself to be successful and I am most happy.

Sue Porter Henderson desires that you too will know success and be happy. She recognizes that every actor is a unique human being not "just another actor." She knows that everyone counts, every single day. She knows that acting is ultimately a people business. It is made up of human beings. It demands humanity. Sue gives it.

Secrets of Successful Actors will help you master your craft, acquire your tools and know success as an actor and perhaps in your life. Read it. Do it. Be it.

You can have the happiness in life you seek without imitating the life you think you want.

If Sue can, you can.

If I did, you shall.

Working Actor Emeritus
The Stainless Steel Magnolia™
Susan Phelps, Ph.D.
November 10, 1998

"To be successful, the first thing to do is fall in love with your work."
Sister Mary Lauretta

"If you work at what you love,
you are successful."
Sue Porter Henderson

Preface

The Successful Actor
Is A *Working* Actor

Getting "*discovered*" or being a "*star*" is a dream of many starting out in the acting profession. For some, achieving stardom is the only acceptable measure of having "made it in the biz." Given the quirky and personal nature of the entertainment business, where talent alone doesn't always count, actors who hold such notions are often disappointed. Moreover, these actors have limited their opportunities for success by narrowing their views about what it means to be successful.

I view success very differently. It is not whether you achieve celebrity status within your chosen profession that determines your professional success. Success is being able to make a living doing what you enjoy. Success is being able to earn an income by doing what you feel passion about. Success is making a living by doing what you love.

If we apply this idea of success to the acting profession, a successful actor is a *working* actor, one who loves to perform and is able to make a living from performing. If you accept my notion of success, as I hope you do, there are many opportunities to work and know success as an actor.

Why This Book?

My name is Sue Porter Henderson. I wrote *Secrets of Successful Actors* to share what *working* actors have learned about what it takes to be successful in the acting business. It contains valuable tips, ideas and resources that will help your acting career no matter what stage of its evolution, starting out, stalled out, or advancing.

I have been a successful *working* actor for over twenty-five years. I am President of Henderson Enterprises, Inc., a New York based company that provides actor support services since 1983 and publishes directories and guides that are of importance to actors who want to work.

I am also a career consultant to actors. In this capacity, I have helped hundreds of actors become successful by getting them focused on the business side of acting. I am honored to be known as the *working* actor's friend.

As an actor, I have worked steadily since 1973 in television and film, including all the major soaps filmed in New York, in support, principal and recurring roles. My screen credits include principal roles in The Bell Jar and The King of Comedy, and roles in The Scout and Ransom. While never a star, I am professionally successful. I continue to be a *working* actor.

My acting career began in 1973, when I arrived in New York City to pursue my dream of becoming a fashion model and actress. At that time, I had few clues about where or how to start and even fewer resources to afford me opportunities to find out. But never underestimate the power of one filled to brimming with unjustified confidence.

Somehow I arrived at the Wilhelmina Agency poised and ready to be discovered. The receptionist there took one look at me and without hesitation informed me of my inadequacies, "you are much too old and way too short." I was at that time twenty-four years old, I remain five feet and seven inches tall.

Just as I was about to let loose the tears, a beautiful woman stepped out of her office. She was Wilhelmina Cooper. She invited me in for a chat. After confirming her receptionist's observations about my lack of suitability for representation by her agency, she proceeded to ask me questions about my career goals and aspirations. Then she explained to me what she believed my career options were and why she thought so.

To make a long story short, she got me focused on my acting interests, particularly soap opera acting. She also introduced me to commercial print modeling, an area of the business about which I knew nothing and a type of modeling for which she felt I was perfect.

In little over a half-hour, Wilhelmina provided me with valuable information and motivated me to go for it. She set me on a good path for the work followed soon thereafter. In short order I became a *working* actor, I knew success. I have never forgotten the impact she had on me and my acting career by encouraging me to continue to pursue my dreams and by giving me the information I needed to do so.

Since 1983, I have helped many actors become successful. This is accomplished by providing actor support services through my company, Henderson Enterprises, Inc. (HEI). From mailing labels to web sites, we help performing artists who seek employment in the competitive field of entertainment.

HEI is founded, managed and operated by *working* actors for *working* actors. Our motto is:

Working Actors Helping Actors Work.

Over the past three years, we have expanded our business to include the much-needed and much-requested personal consultation services. We have also published several industry-related publications, including:

φ   *Henderson's Casting Director's Guide*
φ   *Henderson's Personal Managers Directory*

HEI began simply enough. It was the result of "that bunch of *working* actors sitting around talking on the set." On that day in 1983, "that bunch" talked about those people, places and things that we felt had most contributed to our getting work as actors. We compared experiences, exchanged ideas and swapped our favorite tips and tricks for getting and staying employed as actors. We talked about who worked for who, who knew who and who was who. We discussed who are the best agents, most reliable managers and most active casting directors.

That busy day in 1983 yielded two important outputs. One was the creation of the *Actor's Shoebox.* The other was the creation of the *"IN"* list.

The Actor's Shoebox

The *Actor's Shoebox*, which some of us refer to as "the source," is literally an old shoebox of mine that holds success quips, quotes, tidbits and tips for actors by actors and other industry professionals. We hoped it would become a useful resource for future colleagues and ourselves. We think it has finally become so, given that the box is now full to overflowing.

The *Actor's Shoebox* is presented in the **Resources for Working** Actors section at the end of this book. We loosely organized the material, but elected to leave the ideas and tips we collected from 1983 to 1998 in their original, unedited form. They reflect the mindset, mood-state and mainstay of our professional peers who contributed them.

The *"IN"* List

The other result of that day was the *"IN"* list of those industry people who we knew to be active and interested in discovering and casting talent. We made copies of the list and distributed them to all who were present that day. It became Henderson Enterprises' first mailing list.

In no time at all, others of our actor colleagues heard about the *"IN"* list and wanted it too. We printed it on labels and provided them to any who requested them. Within a few days so many actors requested the labels we decided to charge for them, and so began the business.

Since then, HEI has evolved many actor support products and services, from resume preparation to one-on-one consulting. And the original *"IN"* list that started it all is today known as the Monthly Mailer. Updated regularly, it now averages about 165 active contacts. It remains one of our most popular products.

At the urging of my colleagues and friends, I took responsibility for managing the company that now bears my name. That I was asked to be the one to do so came about for several reasons.

> 1)   I am knowledgeable about organizing and launching a winning marketing campaign. I am after all the daughter of a successful human being. During the course of his professional career, my father was an electronics engineer, a baseball player and a public official. As a public official, my dad held a record for public service by being continuously elected as the

Republican selectman of Raynham, Massachusetts, an office he ultimately held for 36 uninterrupted years. As a father, my dad was always loving and supportive.

I know my dad was successful because even as he neared the end of his life he said, "If I could do it all over again, my profession, my life, my lifestyle, I wouldn't change a thing." Dad made a living working at what he loved and he loved the living he made from his work. The key lessons I take from him are the importance of:

φ Being informed about all aspects of the business in which one seeks employment.

φ Being fair in all interpersonal encounters be they of a business or personal nature.

φ Taking a balanced approach to life, balance professional pursuits with personal lifestyles.

φ Giving because "more is always the result of sharing."

2)   I possess a personality that is desirable of those who manage others, no doubt the result of the training and experience I acquired from twenty-two years as an Eastern Airlines Flight Attendant. I am not given to extremes in mood. While I have the ego required of any ambitious person, I am not egotistical. Nor am I prone to the jealousy that so often hampers other actors from helping their colleagues get work. I am also trustworthy and reliable.

3)   I also have the organizational skills and patience to do what is needed. These I believe were acquired from my mother who was a writer and columnist with a liberal view, and a person who knew how to meet deadlines.

Mom also demonstrated a giving and nonjudgmental approach to all with whom she came in contact. "See who someone is, not who they appear to be, you will see humanity." She was inspiring. I seek to be so for you as well.

As a career consultant, I am privileged to work with my colleagues and fellow actors to impart what I have learned about what it takes to be successful as an actor and in life. No doubt being reared in a stimulating and success-minded environment by caring parents influenced some of my ideas.

The specific ideas presented in this book that relate to acting were acquired over the years from my actor consultation sessions, and from my own experiences as a *working* actor. They reflect the cumulative wisdom of *working* actors, those who have learned what it takes to do what they love, love what they do, and get paid for it.

You may not agree with all the entries in this book. From your own experience, perhaps you could add a few. But if you are new to the business, your career has stalled or you desire to go the next level, the information in this book will enable you to add a business sense of efficiency and direction to your career development.

> *"Challenges make you discover things about yourself, that you never really knew. They are what make the instrument stretch. They are what make you go beyond the norm."*
> **Cicely Tyson**

If you view being successful as a challenge, I challenge you to be successful. I challenge you to be a *working* actor!

If I can, you can.

Working Actor and The *Working* Actor's Friend
Sue Porter Henderson
December 10, 1998
Good luck to you all!

I
Introduction

The *Working* Actor's Success Formula

*"If you don't know where you're going,
any path will do."*
Unknown

*"If you know where you are going,
success may be just around the corner."*
Sue Porter Henderson

Introduction

The *Working* Actor's Success Formula

What you see is a function of where you stand. I have stood beside *working* actors for over twenty-five years as a fellow *working* actor and more recently, also as a business consultant to actors. I believe that the best source of information about what it takes to be successful is to ask successful people. For our purposes here, those successful people are *working* actors.

I have learned that behind every successful actor is a set of experiences that informs and guides his or her future professional actions. Successful actors go with what works and stop doing what does not. In fact, there is a pattern that emerges that suggests the way to success. There is a method to our madness and an identifiable approach we take to getting work as actors. *Working* actors have a formula for achieving success. It is strategic in orientation and dynamic when applied to practice.

The *Working* Actor's Success Formula is three dimensional. It involves a unique way of thinking about:

1) The acting profession—we view it as a business, we call it a craft.

2) The actor within the profession—we view professional actors as suppliers of acting services, we call them one tool of the trade.

3) The actor as a person independent of the profession—we view acting as what actors do, not who they are. When we think of you, we call it view.

Each of these dimensions suggests a course of action for actors to follow and strategies to pursue. It is by understanding this formula and acting on the specific ideas and tips that flow from it that comprise the *Working* Actor's Success Formula. It is what successful actors know. Applied faithfully, this formula will not only help you know success as an actor, I believe it will positively contribute to your overall experience in life.

II
Craft

Acting As a
Business

"Luck is a matter of preparation meeting opportunity."
Oprah Winfrey

"A working actor is a prepared actor who met the opportunity."
Sue Porter Henderson

Craft

Acting As a Business

We often think of a craft as an art, as a description of a creative endeavor over which we seek mastery. By that standard, mastery over the craft of acting is certainly an art. Unfortunately, while many actors practice the craft of acting, few master it to the level of artistry.

Observers of casting practices in the entertainment industry know that having talent can get you noticed, it can even help you get a job. But this assumes that those who hire actors are aware of you and your talent to begin with. More importantly, that they can be motivated to take an interest in discovering what you have to offer them. What makes you unique? Why you versus another actor with whom they are already familiar? How will you be the solution to their next casting problem?

The casting problem is a hiring decision and a management issue. Considered from this vantage, it differs little from the one faced by any professional in any industry who is responsible for identifying, screening and interviewing potential employees on behalf of management. Hiring can involve a whole host of intermediaries from headhunters to employment agencies. In the acting profession, the intermediaries can include agents and managers, as well as casting directors, directors, producers and writers. A casting person's job is to:

> *"Get the right person to do the right job*
> *in the right way at the right time for the*
> *right reason for the right amount of money."*
> **J. Terryl (T. Bubba) Bechtol, CSP**

If you want to be the right actor for the job, you need to think like the *working* actor. That thinking starts with how to think about the acting profession and includes what is meant by craft.

Craft is not limited to a description of a creative activity over which we seek mastery. It refers to any profession, trade or vocation that has in place standards for its practice and expectations for its outcomes. Mastery often involves an entrepreneurial spirit. It requires commitment.

Working actors treat the acting profession as a craft. That craft is the business of acting. The approach they take to its practice is that taken by any person who seeks to master a craft and stay in business.

Apply, Apply, Apply

The measure of a master craftsperson's success lies not in the art with which they practice their craft but in the faithful execution of its science. *Working* actors know when they have mastered their craft because they are actors who work.

> *"The most successful people in life are those who have the best information."*
> **Benjamin Disraeli**

> *"Knowledge is not power. Use of knowledge is power."*
> **J. Terryl (T. Bubba) Bechtol, CSP**

Working actors, like masters of a craft, are continual learners. They are informed, knowledgeable and articulate about who is who and what is what as regards their industry and professional environment. They are current on the relevant issues and trends that effect both the business in which they seek employment and their ability to obtain employment.

Working actors know that having access to the best available information is a key to their success. They also know that knowledge unused is useless. They put their knowledge to work and they get work.

Working actors discover their opportunities by being alert to them, and are therefore prepared to meet them. The *working* actor is a savvy business professional who knows when, where and how to be in the right place at the right time.

"I think the one lesson I have learned is that there is no substitute for paying attention."
Diane Sawyer

Working actors understand what it means to be an actor. They adopt an approach to the acting business that raises their possibilities for employment. They do not seek to be actors, they want to be *working* actors. They are professionals in a professionalized business and they approach it in a business professional manner. They are as aware as they are committed.

Working actors know that talent alone, no matter how unique or special, is not enough to provide the way forward. They know that talent is worth little if no one knows about it. They understand how to promote and market themselves. They know how to network. For them, success at the craft is success at the business.

Working actors have goals to achieve and a process to follow. They are efficient in their practice of the business. They are effective at getting acting work. They know they need to master the business of getting the job before they can have the job they want to get.

Working actors know what help and resources are available to them, how to obtain these resources, and how to use them to their best advantage. They know what they want, who they are, where they are going, why they are going there, how they will get there, who can help get them there. And they know when they have arrived.

Working actors do things right and they do the right things. They are responsible for themselves and respectful to others. They are consistent and persistent in their pursuit of acting work.

Working actors think process, they enact planning. They are ready to work because they are always prepared. They prepare for success by planning for their market entry.

Working actors develop lifestyles and mental attitudes that support them through the tough times and keep them prepared for their opportunities. They adopt mindsets that are lifting to their spirits when life seems low.

Working actors are entrepreneurial and risk-taking by nature. They avail themselves of the latest information and technologies, and they utilize them in their career pursuits. They are not afraid to take risks or to try something new.

"Nothing in life is to be feared.
It is only to be understood."
Marie Curie

Learning your craft is important. Knowing the rules of the business necessary to work at your craft is essential. Acquiring the right tools to practice your craft is critical.

"Be totally well crafted!"
Sue Porter Henderson

III
Tools

The Business
of Acting

"A working actor knows how to obtain professional tools and use them to best advantage. For tools are the means by which we practice our craft, pursue our calling."
Sue Porter Henderson

Tools

The Business of Acting

Every craftsperson needs a set of tools or supplies with which to practice their craft. Tools are the appropriate tangible physical materials necessary to practice any craft. They also include those intangibles such as talent or technique that serve to make one craftsperson better or different from another in the practice and delivery of their craft.

For the master craftsperson, these tools should be the best available that are appropriate to the task. And these tools should be acquired for the least amount of resources, be they time, money or effort. *Working* actor's tools include the money, time and effort required to apply that knowledge.

Effort includes expending energy to obtain the right tools, from interviewing photographers to take that great headshot to finding and taking acting classes with a good teacher. Tools include budgeting, planning and determining what is the minimum amount of resources and effort that can be expended to make a successful entry into the acting business.

> *"No one can arrive from being talented alone.*
> *God gives talent, work transforms talent into genius."*
> **Anna Pavlova**

For *working* actors, tools represent the complete portfolio of what is required for them to:

φ   Be fully informed and knowledgeable about their craft.

φ   Access, develop, prepare and present themselves to the acting profession as professional actors.

Tools of a *Working* Actor's Portfolio

For *working* actors, tangible tools include those materials and services such as headshots, mailers, answering services and acting classes. When actors work on a project, be it a play, television program or film, they are one of many materials that must be molded and shaped to create a unified whole.

The intangible tools of the *working* actor include his or her unique essence, image and talent. Each of these must also be carefully attended to if an actor wants to be a *working* actor.

In this section I describe the specific tools that are needed to obtain work as an actor. I provide success tips that will help you to be efficient in acquiring your tools and effective in utilizing them. I also offer tips and ideas for developing some of your intangibles, those one-of-a-kind aspects of yourself that separate you from the acting pack.

Success Tips for Getting and Staying Informed

There are several ways of acquiring the business knowledge necessary to get your acting career going and to start working as an actor. Reading books such as this one is one way. So are reading the trades, taking classes, or interviewing other successful *working* actors to discover what they know. Other ways range from the less expensive one of being born and reared by *working* actor parents to having experience with the acting business by having been a child actor.

Finally, you can hire a career consultant who acquired professional expertise and knowledge from participating in the acting profession. By hiring a consultant, you are in effect purchasing another person's experience (OPE).

> *"OPE, other people's experience,*
> *if necessary, buy it!"*
> **J. Terryl (T. Bubba) Bechtol, CSP**

Working actors typically use or try most of the ways I mentioned earlier to obtain work over the course of their careers. They stick with those methods that work best for them. Each of these approaches is presented in more detail below.

The Books, The Trades

Reading books about the acting business are a good way to begin to learn what you need to know about the acting business. The beauty of books is that so much information is gathered in a single format and makes this method of knowledge acquisition one of the least cost alternatives. No matter your fiscal condition, access to your acting business knowledge is only a library card away.

There are no disadvantages to reading, ever. What *working* actors concern themselves with is reading a wide selection of books about the acting business, by different authors, that cover various aspects of the business and its people. From reading biographies by and about *working* actors, directors, writers and producers you are able to view the business from multiple perspectives.

Reading historical books about the development and evolution of the business help you understand why the business is organized and operated as it is. Reading industry histories provide insights and explanations about why some aspects of the entertainment business are more or less likely to change than others over time. Acquiring such insights reveal opportunities to work. It is in the gaps that chance often appears.

Starting out, the cleverest *working* actors focus on those areas of the acting business that are more amenable to their participation or suggest some ease for their entry. They also look for opportunities that may have been overlooked by other actors who are so focused on finding instant success that they miss chances to ever discover success.

"Success is a journey, not a destination."
Susan Phelps, Ph.D.

Reading in depth across many areas of the acting business will hone and develop the accuracy of your intuitions. That is, as your knowledge and insight grows about the acting business, so do your opportunities to be a *working* actor. You read situations better, because you have read them many times before. Not only do *working* actors read books, they regularly devour "the trades" of the entertainment industry.

The trades is business slang for trade publications (daily, weekly or monthly) that provide industry specific information and bring attention to items of interest to industry players. The trades is slang in many industries.

In the acting business, the trades are many. Among the better known are *Back Stage, The Hollywood Reporter* and *Variety.*

Back Stage is a New York focused weekly, nationally distributed. In addition to news, classifieds and advertisements, it posts casting notices and audition announcements — job opportunities *working* actors do not miss. *Back Stage West* is a sister publication, which provides similar information for actors in Los Angeles.

The Hollywood Reporter is nationally distributed in a number of formats. It is of particular appeal to actors interested in working on films. It contains information about films in preparation and development, suggesting ways *working* actors might get in on the ground floor of a forthcoming project.

Variety is a nationally distributed weekly. It covers a broad spectrum of the acting business of interest to both actors and investors.

Working actors know that wherever a viable community of actors and entertainers is found, so too is a trade of specific interest to them. The two main interests are regional or specialty. For example, *Reel* is a regional trade that covers the acting business for actors who work in or near Wilmington, North Carolina. Other trades focus on entertainment specialties. No matter your performance interests, magic, comedy, drama or dance, a trade exists for you. Search them out. Read them.

Take a Class, Interview an Actor

Taking classes on or about the acting business can be valuable. *Working* actors tend to prefer short seminars that provide cutting edge information that is immediately applicable to their situation. Formal course work such as that taken in a college or university is important to your development, particularly as it develops your general business awareness. But once you are active in the acting business—once you are a *working* actor—you need relevant information. You need it now.

> *"Never let your schooling*
> *interfere with your education."*
> **Mark Twain**

Interview and network with other *working* actors. Ask them questions about who they know. How have they approached the business? What have they found to work best for them? If you want to work, make time to discover what other successful *working* actors know.

To jump-start your acting career, consider hiring a consultant! Many *working* actors have found that buying the experience of a consultant is a major contribution to their success and view the consultant as an asset. If you can afford it, before setting out, hire a career consultant, one who is knowledgeable of the acting business.

As your career evolves, so do your informational needs, your goals and the nature of the problems or concerns that you confront. *Working* actors periodically employ consultants or hire expertise throughout their careers. They buy the expertise of one who is best suited to help them overcome a current problem or reach their latest goal.

A consultant can dramatically speed the rate at which an actor is ready and able to work. He or she can also concentrate their energies on identifying those intangibles and unique aspects of an individual actor. A consultant can then share those observations and provide direction to the actor in a one-on-one personal session. This information is valuable and rarely available in any other way.

For example, how do you know what your image or type is if not told so by one who knows? You can be told to get a great headshot, but how will you know it is great? What is unique about you? What will separate you from the pack or differentiate you from the crowd?

As a rule, unless they are active in the entertainment business, family and friends are generally not the best referent point for this type of career advice and counsel. Granted, such advice is cheaper and easier to stomach, but it is rarely useful for getting it together as a *working* actor.

> *"In consulting, as in life, you get what you pay for, you get what you reward. Reward yourself, find and pay for a good consultant!"*
> **The Stainless Steel Magnolia** ™
> **Susan Phelps, Ph.D.**

What a consultant can save you in future time, effort and expense is well worth it if it is the right consultant. The right consultant is easier to discover than you may imagine.

The best consultants are those who have good reputations for delivering the services and assistance they said they could and would. They are able to do so because they possess the experience based knowledge you need.

Reputation is learned through word-of-mouth. If you want a good consultant, ask your professional *working* actor colleagues who advised them. A good consultant usually acquires their knowledge from personal experience. In effect, they have made the mistakes they will try to prevent you from repeating. To speed up your career, they tell you what experience has taught them about being successful.

It is generally easier and less expensive in the long run to employ the services of a consultant. Why struggle through the process when a consultant can shave years off your learning curve? Economists refer to this type of efficiency or savings, as reducing your opportunity cost of spending time, energy and money elsewhere.

Many *working* actors compare the education they acquire by hiring a good career consultant to that they would have received by taking months, if not years, of schooling from a choice university or a college of their choice. Others rate their experience as more valuable because the advice they receive is usually more timely and accurate. It is information from one who does or has done what the actor seeks to do, not from one who wants to do that, without having been there. For almost all, a meeting with a good consultant is an efficient and effective tool for getting on path and staying the course.

Working Actors and Their Acting Training

Working actors think of themselves and their talent as commodities or products to be marketed, promoted and sold to the entertainment trade. In effect, *working* actors understand that they are suppliers of acting services and are the principal tool of the acting trade.

> *"Creative minds have always been known to survive any kind of bad training."*
> **Anna Freud**

To work, the actor constructs, develops and presents his or herself to the best possible affect. In doing so, actors are required to employ sets of complementary tools to enhance their value and fill purchasers' needs.

Acting technique, for example, is a technology of the acting profession. It is a means of presenting the self in an audition and a means of practicing the profession. It is an acquired skill. It can sometimes substitute for talent in cases where it may be lacking.

Auditions and showcases are two ways that actors have to demonstrate their abilities and readiness for an acting job. Audition centers (where you can pay to audition for agents and casting directors) are well known among *working* actors.

Marketing and Promotion

If you want the people that hire or those that screen in or out actors to be considered for hiring, you have to be "in it to win it." You have to let the right people know you exist and where and how they can reach you. To let them know you exist involves marketing and self-promotional activities.

Actors who then wish to be contacted by an interested party to whom they marketed will possess communication equipment, such as answering machines, beepers, etc. Carrier pigeons were swept away by the last wave.

Unions

There are four major unions that have potential importance to a professional actor or entertainer. Whether you can, will or should hold membership in any or all of them during the course of your career depends on your acting interests and opportunities. The four major performer unions are:

φ *American Federation of Television and Radio Artists,* (AFTRA). AFTRA represents actors for live or video taped television programs including radio, movies, soap operas, voice (audio) recordings and voice work in commercials, including singers. For more information call the union directly or check their web site at: http://www.aftra.org. Anyone can join AFTRA.

It is an open union which means membership requirements are lenient. In short, if you can afford the initiation fee and pay the semi-annual dues, membership is yours.

φ *Actors Equity Association,* (AEA). AEA represents legitimate theater performers and has restrictions about how it is joined. To find out the current requirements for membership, call the union directly or check their web site at: http://www.actorsequity.org.

φ *American Guild of Variety Artists,* (AGVA). AGVA represents artists in the variety entertainment field such as comedians, singers, and dancers. Its present jurisdiction includes performers in Broadway, Off-Broadway, Cabaret productions, night club entertainers and theme park performers. The Guild has several long-term collective bargaining agreements with Radio City Music Hall, Disneyland and Universal Studios Hollywood. Anyone can join AGVA. It is an open union which means membership requirements are lenient. In short, if you can afford the initiation fee and pay the tri-annual dues, membership is yours. For more information call the union directly (The national office is located in New York (212) 675-1003.).

φ *Screen Actors Guild,* (SAG). SAG is the union for film performance and represents the union membership most sought after by actors. It is also a membership that is more difficult to obtain. Actors who appear in

SAG signatory movies, television programs or commercials must be members of SAG. To find out the current requirements for membership call them directly or check their web site at: http://www.sag.com.

The distinction between union signatory movies, television programs and commercials governed by AFTRA versus SAG is a technical one. When the medium on which the entertainment is recorded is film, it is under SAG jurisdiction, when it is video, it is under AFTRA. The rationale for this distinction is rooted in the history and evolution of the entertainment industry and related technologies. It is also a history that an informed actor will one day choose to read. (As we go to press, AFTRA and SAG members are voting on the merger of both unions.)

It is neither necessary nor always desirable for the beginning actor to belong to a performers union. Granted, union affiliation can make an actor feel as if he or she is a member of the acting profession. But there are many opportunities to work as a non-union performer, even in New York, Los Angeles and Chicago.

Moreover, union membership can be a drawback to the beginning actor who should be focused on gaining professional experience versus having a professional union credential. Further, if you are an actor or aspiring actor who resides outside of the big three: New York, Los Angeles or Chicago, you may be surprised at the number of non-union opportunities to work as a professional actor that exist in your own backyard. Union membership in these instances will usually be unnecessary to avail yourself of the opportunities you uncover. It can also be a liability because of the expense you incur for membership when it is unnecessary.

Membership Does Have Its Privileges

If you are a member of any or all of the performers unions, AFTRA, AEA, AGVA or SAG, you have access to cutting edge information about acting job opportunities. Become fully aware and avail yourself of the insider information about casting notices and related job opportunities and postings that are obtainable because of your union affiliations. Specifically, call your union hotlines regularly.

If you are a member of the film performers union, *Screen Actors Guild,* (SAG), you can and should be listed in the *Academy Players Directory*. A listing in this directory provides another way to market and promote yourself.

Network, Network, Network

In the entertainment industry as in most other industries, who you know can matter more than what you know. It is also true that if you have an "in" with the right people, the less strictly you must observe job seeking protocol.

Your connections enhance your ability to find and have an opportunity to be a *working* actor. The need for marketing tools such as pictures, resumes and demo tapes as well as the requirement to engage in extensive self-promotional activities are also lessened. In short, the better your acting industry contacts and the stronger your connections to them, the more you save in terms of money, time and effort in getting acting work. Moreover, you not only work more often, you often get better acting work, choicer roles and longer employment contracts.

The experience gained from performing in better acting roles helps you get better as an actor. It may even make you act better. This latter better is the best better benefit you give your friends and colleagues who found your state of unemployment pitiful.

Opportunities to network are many and often. The limits are only those placed on you by your unique circumstances or those you place upon yourself by limiting your creativity.

Be Ready, Be Prepared

Regardless of your contacts and connections, *working* actors are ready actors. They understand the quirky nature of the business that can have them out of a job before it even starts. They understand the need to be entrepreneurial in their pursuit of acting work. They are ready to respond to the one-of-a-kind opportunities that seem to be everywhere when one is alert, when one is paying attention and when one is thinking success. They are ready because they are prepared to be.

Being prepared means prepared to work as an actor or to work at getting acting work. It involves keeping your promotional package up-to-date and having audition material ready to present, such as monologues or songs.

If you are starting out or are lesser known than you would like to be, then your promotional package may be the place to begin to get prepared, to be ready to be a *working* actor. It must be well crafted and the best you can afford. It should be designed to be winning.

At a minimum, the elements of a winning promotional package include an up-to-date, properly formatted theatrical resume attached to the back of a head shot or 3/4 shot that shows a real, approachable you. Both the resume and the photo are 8x10. The photos are matte or semi-matte finished, never glossy. If the package is to be mailed, it always contains a cover letter.

The mailer is designed to fit its contents. It is addressed completely. *Working* actors avoid return to sender episodes by ensuring that there is enough postage to get the package to its final destination.

At a maximum and only when requested by agents or casting directors, a winning promotional package may also include a demo-tape. It can sometimes include a photo composite (such as for work as a print actor) or some other special request materials.

A Winning Promotional Strategy

Once you have the elements of a winning promotional package the next step is to get you and it out there so you can obtain opportunities to audition and to get acting work. To accomplish this, it is useful if those in positions to hire you actually receive your package. *Working* actors make sure to send packages on a continuous basis. We said it before and we say it again: what good is your talent, tools or technique if no one knows about them?

Working actors follow a winning promotional strategy. At any given point in time, use your promotional package to:

φ   Show what you look like and how you photograph.
φ   Tell who you are and what you have accomplished as an actor.
φ   Indicate your readiness and availability for acting work.

Over time your package can become a way for you to:

φ   Create name recognition for yourself.
φ   Advertise and showcase your accomplishments.
φ   Build your credibility as a responsible and dedicated actor to those who hire.

The above three opportunities result from following a winning promotional strategy, one which requires you to be accurate, reliable and timely in getting and staying in touch:

φ   With the right people.

φ   At the right times.

φ   In the right ways.

The right people are those who currently hold jobs that allow them to hire actors directly such as casting directors or those who serve as intermediaries (such as agents or managers) to screen actors for their appropriateness to be considered for a given entertainment project. They are also the "in" people, depending on whom you talk to.

The right times are as soon as a new entertainment project has been announced, as soon as you hear about casting for any project, or by following a regular schedule of notifying the right people of your availability and accomplishments, usually via mail.

The right ways are always the ways of the right people. It is their way or the highway. *Working* actors understand this. To know who the right people are and how to contact them, the *working* actor will:

φ   Talk with other *working* actors about how and from whom they got their most recent acting work.
φ   Review industry casting and production who's who guides and directories.

The best casting guides and directories are updated regularly. They track changes in casting and production personnel and provide both contact information and specifics about how actors who wish to work may contact them. The better-known industry who's who guides, directories and trades of interest to actors are:

φ *Henderson's Casting Director Guide - New York Edition*

φ *Henderson's Personal Managers Directory - USA*

φ *The New York Edition of The Agencies*

φ *The Hollywood Edition of The Agencies*

φ *Ross Reports - New York and Los Angeles*

φ *Breakdown Services - Hollywood Casting Directors Guide*

φ *Academy Players Directory - USA*

φ *Black Talent News - USA*

φ *Chicago Creative Directory*

φ *Regional Theater Directory - USA*

φ *The Actors Guide - Southeast*

φ *Theatrical Index - USA*

φ *Variety - USA*

To stay in touch with the right people, *working* actors keep and maintain an up-to-date contact list or database. They purchase contacts or labels from actor support service providers, such as from my company, Henderson Enterprises, Inc. To know when a project is being cast, who is casting it, and how to get submitted to audition for it, the *working* actor will:

φ Research, Research, Research.
φ Network, Network, Network.
φ Market, Market, Market.

If the above three are done right, an actor may land an audition. The *working* actor will have existing audition material, such as a monologue or song, and will:

φ Prepare, Prepare, Prepare.
φ Practice, Practice, Practice.
φ Perfect, Perfect, Perfect.

Working actors know that if they so choose, there exist opportunities to network and make connections every day. They market themselves regularly by:

φ Doing mailings.
φ Making phone calls.
φ Taking auditions or interviews.

Working actors know that agents, casting directors and managers seldom answer their own phones and rarely open their doors to new actors unless introduced. Let's hear it again for the value of networking.

Working actors also know that agents, casting directors and managers:

φ Do open their mail.
φ Need you as much as you need them.

Organize Your Life, Free Up Time, Know About Money

Working actors are organized and orderly. They know they must manage their time so it won't manage them. They record their appointments as soon as they are able after they receive them.

Working actors avoid using their memory to store dates and times. They prefer to save the empty space for entertaining more creative ideas and indulging more thoughtful pursuits.

Working actors are on time for professional appointments. They are never no-shows, unless they are deceased. They rarely cancel.

Working actors manage their professional activities in a professional business manner. They know how to budget their spending, track their expenditures, maintain and prepare their business records for meetings with an accountant or heaven forbid, the IRS.

To manage their time and money, *working* actors:

φ Own some type of professional planner or scheduling device in which to record their appointments and note their spending.
φ More importantly, they actually use it.

The bottom-line on bottom-lines for *working* actors is:

> *"Good things come to those who wait*
> *Great things come to those who hustle."*
> **Unknown**

IV
View

You,
the *Working* Actor

*"The richer you are in human experience,
the fewer acting classes you will need."*
**The Stainless Steel Magnolia™
Susan Phelps, Ph.D.**

*"Where talent leads is not always
where one supposes."*
**Sue Porter Henderson
The *Working* Actor's Friend**

View

You, the *Working* Actor

The happiest *working* actors that I have known are those who believe themselves to be successful human beings who happen to be professional actors. What you believe is who you are and is revealed in how you act, react and respond to the variety of people, places and situations that you will encounter over the course of your life. If you believe you can be successful you will be. If you think you are, you are. What you believe in is your reality.

"You become who you think you are. But don't confuse who you are as a person with what you do for a living."
J. Terryl (T. Bubba) Bechtol, CSP

In this section I offer *working* actors ideas for balancing life and career. These are success tips for keeping you in view. They represent what *working* actors know about getting and staying happy, healthy and motivated.

Attitude Is Everything!

If what you believe is your reality, then your attitude is everything. What you think about effects how you feel about yourself, others and your prospects in life. Understanding who you are as a person and learning how to balance what you do for a living is the key to having a happy and healthy life.

*"No pessimist ever discovered the secrets
of the stars, or sailed to an uncharted land,
or opened a new heaven to the human spirit."*
Helen Keller

Working actors develop lifestyles and mental attitudes that support them through the tough times and keep them prepared and ready to make and meet their opportunities. They adopt mindsets that are lifting to their spirits when their life may seem low.

Working actors strive to keep a positive outlook even in the worst of times. For where there is hope, there is opportunity. There is creativity. There is a future. There is always a second chance. They know that to keep the you in view, they must find balance in life. They must maintain their perspective.

*"Once in a lifetime opportunities come
along every single day."*
**The Stainless Steel Magnolia™
Susan Phelps, Ph.D.**

"Nobody can make you feel inferior
without your consent."
Eleanor Roosevelt

Balance, Balance, Balance

Working actors believe that keeping the you in view mandates that we strive to strike a balance between what we do for a living with who we are as individuals. It is a goal that supports a particular mind set and lifestyle that positively contributes to our overall experience in life. It is a perspective that says I know who I am. I am not what I do.

To find your balance, you need to think broadly about youself, your life and the meaning of your career within it. To do so requires that you schedule time for yourself to think. It demands that you care for yourself physically, mentally and emotionally. For if you take time for yourself and to care for yourself, you just may discover yourself. If you do, you may find pathways to opportunities that you could never have imagined.

"We need time to dream, time to remember,
and time to reach the infinite. Time to be."
Gladis Taber

"If you don't occasionally get 'carried away'
you may be 'carted away'!"
The Stainless Steel Magnolia™

From my experiences as both a *working* actor and as a consultant to actors, I believe that being successful is a choice you can make. It is a lifestyle option.

Going for balance encourages us to develop multiple dimensions of ourselves. From developing and discovering our inner resources to acquiring additional, non-acting related skills. Expanding the mind and exploring other aspects of ourselves is of value, whether you make acting your only profession or choose to pursue other careers as your life evolves.

It is important to avoid allowing your career to become the only area in which you are conversant. When you do so, it is taking the idea of specializing to an extreme that at best will annoy others at worst limit your professional opportunities, because you've stunted your personal growth.

> *"If you're not what you do, do you*
> *know what your life is about?"*
> **Susan Phelps, Ph.D.**

Happy *working* actors are outgoing in their efforts to be informed and knowledgeable about the world around them. They cultivate interests, hobbies, and friends outside their profession. They seek to develop themselves as total human beings. They wish to be well-rounded.

Take a good hard look at yourself and your life, examine the role of your career within them and its impact on each.

*"I always felt that who you are as a human being
is more important than success in the theater.
You have to live a full life. Otherwise, you
won't have anything to bring to the theater."*
Marjorie Lord

Acting is an instance where all work and no play can lead to an imbalance in the personality and make you a bore. It can also limit your opportunities to grow in the profession as a professional actor because you have focused on acting at the expense of growing the self.

I believe that if you attempt to lead a balanced life, some of your acting training needs will become lessened over time. For over time, you will have had the life experiences you are trying to learn how to simulate.

Take care of yourself! We often work so hard at trying to obtain what we think we want that we neglect ourselves, our health, our family and our friends.

The happiest *working* actors I have known have discovered themselves. What is unique about you? What are your unique gifts and talents? Discover them. Mine them, no matter how lengthy or painful the process. You will know when it is time to display them.

*"Everyone has talent. What is rare is the courage to
follow the talent to the dark place where it leads."*
Erica Jong

*"I didn't belong as a kid, and that always
bothered me. If only I'd known that one
day my differences would be an asset, then
my early life would have been much easier."*
Bette Midler

Feed your soul. Energize your spirit. Be kind to yourself by giving to others. Many *working* actors enjoy the feelings of accomplishment, caring and contribution they get by helping others.

"It's never crowded along the extra mile."
Unknown

One way to stay in tune with yourself is by giving back to society, by helping others and by being a good friend. Seek out ways to help in the community. Volunteer and serve. Be philanthropic with your time. Be that friend that walks into the room when the rest of the world has walked out. Help your colleagues, friends and peers. Remember that your collective opportunities to work as an actor is expanded by helping other actors obtain work.

*"I am not afraid of storms, for I am
learning how to sail my ship."*
Louisa May Alcott

"Life is a journey.
Embrace it.
Go the distance.
Believe in yourself.
For if you do not,
why should anyone else?"
The Stainless Steel Magnolia™
Susan Phelps, Ph.D.

"If my success is to be, it is up to me!"
Sue Porter Henderson
The *Working* Actor's Friend

V
Resources
For *Working* Actors

Resource A:

Tools of the Trade

The Actor's Shoebox

Below is presented the *Actor's Shoebox*. It is a loosely organized collection of the favorite quips, tips and ideas of those who have learned how to get and stay employed as actors. These were collected between 1983 and 1998 from our professional peers, *working* actors and industry personnel. We present them in their original, unedited form reflecting the mindset, mood-state and mainstay of the individuals who contributed them.

The Tools

Pictures

1. You must have one great 8x10 straight-on picture, full face headshot or 3/4 shot. Children need 4x6 snapshots.

2.   Your headshot must show a real, approachable you.

3.   Research various photographers you've heard or read about in the trades. Be sure to ask other actors who shot their pictures.

4.   Reproduction houses generally have a headshot photographer guide that allows you to view the work of many photographers all at once.

5.   Always meet with photographers in advance. Examine their work. See how well you get along and then decide who you feel most comfortable with before booking your appointment.

6.   The shots to be done, the price, makeup, hair, your wardrobe and backgrounds should be discussed with your photographer prior to your session.

7.   Select proper clothes and colors for your photographs.

8.   Avoid wearing fancy jewelry or wild prints.

9.   Women need a makeup and hair stylist.

10. Men need pressed powder to avoid shine.

11. Men should be clean-shaven. (Hair-cuts 2 weeks prior to shoot)

12. You must look like your pictures. Don't airbrush your pictures to glamorize yourself.

13. Your selection of pictures must represent work you can realistically get. Know your type and how to develop it.

14. Show your proofs/contact sheets to agents and friends before final selections are made.

15. Ask for referrals of good reproduction companies. Ask other actors who they use and why.

16. Order your pictures in matte or semi matte finish. Never glossy.

17. You need postcards, save money by using a printing process instead of a photographic process.

18. Choose a friendly smiling shot for your postcard.

19. If you can portray various characters, send a postcard with several photos (also referred to as a composite)

Resumes and Envelopes

20. Use proper theatrical format for your resume.

21. Print your resume on white or off-white paper.

22. Make sure your resume can be read clearly.

23. Use a picture resume to let industry people see two different pictures.

24. Proofread your resume several times before duplicating.

25. Never lie on your resume.

26. Have resume cut to fit your 8x10. If it is changing rapidly you should only print a limited amount.

27. Attach your picture to your resume before you leave home.

28. Use a glue stick or 4 staples to attach your picture to your resume or have it professionally done.

29. You can add several new credits to your printed resume in ink (draws attention to new credits).

30. Use envelopes, any color, that properly fit your 8x10 pictures. (You do not need cardboard.)

31. Don't use oversized clasp envelopes with additional tape, they're difficult to open.

Cover Letters

32. Always include a brief cover letter with your picture and resume. Begin by stating what type of work you are interested in obtaining.

33. You can typeset or hand write your cover letters. If you are currently appearing in something, mention it in your cover letter.

34. Cover letters are short, sweet and to the point.

35. Sign your cover letters.

36. Remember that ignorance costs money and jobs.

Acting Schools and Teachers

37. Start training before mailing. Learn your art. Know your craft.

38. Audit or research any class, school or teacher you are considering working with.

39. Keep your lighthouse on.

40. Be cautious of any high-pressure sales tactics, costly package deals or one-stop shopping schools.

41. Good teachers with legitimate teaching skills will come up in conversation when talking to other industry people.

42. Some of the best acting schools are colleges, but some independent acting schools are credible. Research!

43. If you don't know if acting is for you, it might be a good idea to start with a commercial class, then meet commercial agents.

44. Read plays.

45. Be strong enough to handle criticism.

46. There are no mistakes, only lessons.

47. Acting is not a business for thin-skinned people.

48. Know how to tell anyone about yourself in 90 seconds, in 60 is even better.

49. Learn how to audition.

50. Before you meet agents, have several one-minute mono-
    logues available that demonstrate your ability and range.

Answering Service

51. The phone is the actor's lifeline to work.

52. Actors must have a reliable answering service, voice-
    mail system, cell phone or beeper.

53. You must have a professional message on your
    answering machine.

54. Actors need to be reachable within an hour.

55. Answer the phone with enthusiasm and energy in your
    voice. If you can't, let the service answer it.

56. If you don't live in the city you want to work in, use
    that city's local answering services or get an 800 number.

57. Check your service regularly, at least every hour.

58. Make sure a phone number appears on your resume and
    postcard.

The Internet

59. Learn about internet access in books or at your local
    public library.

60. Some casting directors and agents use the internet to find their talent.

61. Advertise yourself on the internet. Get your own web site and list it on your resume.

62. *Back Stage* is now published on the internet. Visit: http://www.backstage.com.

63. Check out *Henderson's Talent Registry*, http://www.8x10s.com.

64. *Playbill Online* has some casting notices and other acting information, http://www.playbill.com.

65. For casting information online, log onto the Breakdown Services web-site, http://www.breakdownservices.com. Then select Actors Access.

66. Check out http://www.actingworld.com for acting related services and information.

Mailings and Marketing

67. Market! Market! Market!

68. Follow-up with postcards and thank you notes.

69. Send showcase flyers, highlight your name.

70. Send any good reviews you receive. Highlight your name.

71. Once a year, your 8x10s should be sent to selected agents, managers and all active casting directors.

72. Casting directors cast what they are hired to cast.

73. Utilize *Henderson Mailing Labels* to get your mailings done accurately and efficiently.

74. Be acquainted with the Film Guide in *The Hollywood Reporter*.

75. Know how to read the *Theatrical Index* and how to submit yourself for the projects mentioned.

76. Any actor can send an 8x10 and resume to any casting person even if the actor is not a union member.

> *"Build credibility, do follow up mailings."*
> **John "Jes" Stephens, *Working* Actor**

77. Do not mail your photo and resume to a city unless you plan to spend extended time there or can easily and quickly travel to that location.

78. The breaks you're looking for will be the result of talent and hard work.

79. Casting directors, agents and personal managers do open their mail. Remember: they need you!

80. You can send or drop off pictures and resumes at theaters if addressed to a specific contact.

81. Actors should always have their photo and information in the *Academy Players Directory* used by film and TV casting people on both coasts.

82. Know how to organize your career and treat it as a business.

83. Know what print work is and how to submit for it.

84. Most of all don't get bogged down with mailings. Keep it simple, get it done. If this is a problem for you, utilize a reputable actor mailing service.

85. Audition notices for showcases appear frequently in the trade papers.

86. Agents and casting people are more likely to attend Equity approved showcases.

87. A scene-night is usually an evening of scenes performed for industry people. Get involved.

88. There are audition centers available where you can pay to audition for agents and casting directors.

89. When casting directors, agents and personal managers say "Don't phone, fax or visit," they mean it.

Interviews and Auditions

90. Be prepared for whatever you are auditioning for.

91. Do not take criticisms personally.

92. Write down all your appointments.

93. A balanced life makes a more interesting person. Have a life outside the business.

94. Stay focused and motivated.

95. Learn how to handle rejection.

96. Don't let negativity shut you down.

97. As a general rule, never call agents or casting directors unless you are returning a call.

98. If you can avoid it, never call an agent on Mondays.

99. When departing from a meeting with an agent, ask for the best way to keep in touch.

100. Be yourself. Figure out what that means and go for it.

101. Be positive and enthusiastic about your work.

102. Casting directors want you to be good.

103. Talk slow, think quick.

104. Dress appropriately for interviews. Do not go overboard.

105. Make audition material shine.

106. Remember the names of people you meet.

107. Remove sunglasses when being interviewed.

108. Don't think industry people know all the answers, they do not.

109. Think total career and long term. What is right for one actor at a given point in time may not be right for another.

110. Know how to use your eyes. Have a realistic sense of who you are.

111. Learn how to do cold readings well.

112. Don't try to learn everything at once.

113. Learn how to take directions well.

114. Work on your ability to memorize lines.

115. Be aware of what is happening around you.

116. Remember, acting is reacting.

117. Stay connected to yourself.

118. Make a commitment to your work.

119. Seize every opportunity for additional training.

120. Know the players.

121. Ask questions. Listen to the answers.

122. Audition pieces for actors are about 2 1/2 minutes in length. For singers, 16 to 32 bars.

123. Look at commercials, there is much to be learned.

124. Learn by watching others.

125. If acting on sitcoms is among your goals, watch them.

126. See films. Study the work of actors you respect.

127. If you are interested in soap operas, watch them.

128. Take a specialized class dedicated to soap opera acting.

129. Read and look at the pictures in soap opera publications.

130. Be open-minded and flexible in the growing process.

131. If running late, call to let the person know. If you must cancel, cancel.

132. "Please" and "Thank-you" are never out-of-line.

133. Be diplomatic when promoting yourself.

134. Do not interrupt people.

135. Listen, then respond.

136. Do not shake hands with people if you have a cold.

137. Learn to take directions well.

138. Human touch is important to all creative people.

139. Do not chew gum in interviews or auditions.

140. Stage directors look for an actor who can act his way into the part. Film directors look for an actor who happens to fill the part.

141. Write "Thank-you" notes for interviews and jobs.

142. Never go on an audition under the influence of alcohol or drugs.

143. Smile.

144. Show respect for everyone with whom you come in contact. Today's receptionist could be tomorrow's producer.

145. Do not give expensive gifts to agents or casting directors for work/auditions, etc.

146. Be optimistic.

147. Develop charisma.

148. Read, understand. If you don't understand, ask questions.

149. Be able to recall which agents and casting directors know your work or have met you before.

150. See theatrical productions and be able to talk about them at any replacement auditions you might consider attending.

151. Know that casting directors, agents, and personal managers only receive money when you work. No money "up front" to anyone!

152. Modeling is acting.

153. Practice! Practice! Practice!

154. Always arrive at least 10 minutes before your scheduled audition time to prepare.

155. If you make a mistake during an audition, simply ask to please start again.

156. Don't change anything at a call back audition.

157. Auditioning can be very stressful, but try to relax and be yourself.

158. Audition for everything you can, then decide what kind of career you want.

159. Buy the trade papers, check *Back Stage* the day it arrives.

160. The way you read should demonstrate your range of talent and readiness for important roles.

161. When you have experience working with industry "names," let those names come out in an interview.

162. In commercial auditions, look directly at the copy board or cue card. It will look like you are talking to the viewer and you can see the lines.

163. Know what the word "take" means.

164. Bring your "self" to the role. Do not over-prepare.

165. Control body movements when auditioning on and off camera.

166. Do not step on other actors' lines.

167. An actor needs more than talent, he needs to fill the room with a presence.

Finding an Agent, Casting Director or Manager

168. Know where, when and how to showcase your talents.

169. Be assertive without turning people off.

170. Learn how to build credibility.

171. Ask friends to help you meet agents, casting directors, managers, etc.

172. Take a class that brings in agents for you to meet or provides opportunities for you to audition for them.

173. Keep in touch after meetings and auditions.

174. If you're new to the business, your agent is you.

175. Agents need to see that you are committed to your work.

176. Persistence is one of the most important characteristics an actor can develop.

177. If an agent, casting director or manager requests that you use a certain photographer or reproduction house in order for them to consider you, run the other way.

178. That stuff everybody says about "who you know" is true.

179. Mail! Getting agents, casting directors and personal managers interested is essential.

180. An actor must be signed to an agent in Los Angeles to be submitted for work.

181. If an actor wants to do principal roles in films without strong stage credits, the best place to do so is Los Angeles.

182. Volunteer for union committees etc. It is great for networking and career advancement.

183. If you want to do principal film work in New York, it helps to have theater credits, a great manager, exceptional credibility, connections and some luck.

184. Personal managers sometimes take new people they can develop. Know who they are, what they want and what they can do for your career.

185. Know the difference between a manager, a publicist and a business lawyer.

186. Read *Henderson's Personal Managers Directory,* everything you need to know about Personal Managers.

187. Support groups for actors are available for help along the way.

188. Before signing with a personal manager, find out what agents he works with and if he has daily access to breakdown services

189. Agents get 10% of an actor's pay. Managers generally get 15% to 20%.

190. Never sign contracts with blank spaces.

191. All agents are not alike. For the good jobs, an actor needs a franchised agent.

192. Agents need to know you exist. Build your credibility one step at a time. Keep them informed.

193. Check *The Academy Players Directory* and see who manages the top performers.

194. An agent's job is to get you the best roles, billing and salary possible.

195. If you are signed with an agent, don't seek a personal manager without talking to your agent.

196. A recommendation from an industry related person could help you get an agent or a personal manager.

197. Don't worry about getting into the unions. If the director or the producer wants you for principal work, a waiver will be obtained.

About Audio and Video Tapes

198. Do not send out unsolicited tapes.

199. Putting your picture on your audition tape cover makes it more appealing and encourages viewing.

200. If you have an audition tape, indicate that fact on your resume.

201. Your videotape for film and TV should be no longer than seven (7) minutes in length, presented on 1/2" cassettes. Ideal audition tape is made up of short clips about one (1) minute each, showing your talents in different areas.

202. Your videotape for commercials can be 3 or 4 minutes in length and should be separated from your film work.

203. Have your tape professionally edited.

Working as an Actor

204. Leave valuables at home.

205. Never be a "no-show."

206. Never tell an industry person you are on vacation. If you cannot accept an audition or job, simply say you are booked.

207. Always ask questions about makeup, hair and wardrobe in advance.

208. Turn off cell phone and beepers on sets.

209. Never cancel a booking unless you or a family member dies.

210. Don't disappear from a set unless you clear it with the stage manager or assistant.

211. Sign your name and print your social security number clearly on work vouchers.

212. Always try to bring appropriate wardrobe and comfortable shoes to the set.

213. Do not take food from the craft tables unless you are going to eat it.

214. If you do not enjoy the work, do not accept the job.

215. If you have any problems, communicate with the assistant director or stage manager. Never leave the set without permission.

216. Always be polite and professional.

217. Never say you can do something you can not do to get the job.

218. Maintain your sense of humor.

219. Understudying can be a valuable job and a great learning experience.

220. Realize "temp work" or the like are means to an end. It pays necessary bills and funds your acting career.

221. If you have an agent, he or she will handle contracts or payment for work.

222. Remember the 3 R's: Respect for self, Regard for others, Responsibility for your actions in life.

223. Do not audition for an agent until you feel you can do what is required.

224. Talent alone is not enough, find something special to promote yourself or to help your agent or personal manager promote you.

225. Radiate yourself and do not try to intimidate anyone. Be confident that your personality is unique.

226. Do not worry about the words in the film script. They are not as important as your image on the screen.

227. Do not let obstacles stand in the way of reaching your goals.

228. See a lot of films for professional development. (Movies are tax deductible when going for this reason)

229. Learn the difference between an agent, a casting director and a personal manager.

230. If you have only a few good credits, seek a small agency.

231. Do not beg for work, but you may ask.

Miscellany

232. Start from the present.

233. Set realistic goals, then over achieve.

234. Be part of your community.

235. Read the headlines everyday. Be informed, know what is going on.

236. Do something for your career everyday.

237. Life is sometimes not the dance of joy, realize you have to make your own music.

238. Use your time efficiently.

239. Do not do anything illegal.

240. Do not write checks unless you can cover them.

241. Go the extra mile.

242. Be realistic.

243. Learn to laugh at yourself.

244. Develop a sense of humor if you don't have one.

245. Self-discipline is the key to success.

246. Be flexible.

247. Do everything in moderation.

248. Distance yourself from greed of any kind.

249. Avoid negative people.

250. Be aware of scams. Do not be a victim.

251. Take fewer things seriously.

252. Share.

253. Be pleasant to everyone.

254. Be organized.

255. File your taxes.

256. Keep records and receipts.

257. Have a good accountant that understands the acting business.

258. Pick up after yourself.

259. Do not judge people prematurely.

260. Do not exhibit prejudice against any race or lifestyle.

261. Always be on time.

262. Know how to listen.

263. If your home surroundings are affecting your work, seek to make a positive environmental change.

264. Have a clean, well-lit and organized space in which to live.

265. Share your knowledge.

266. If you are right for a job you will get it.

267. Buy and use a professional planner to record your appointments and spending.

268. Realize that achieving fame does not guarantee happiness.

269. Know what is going on around you. There is greatness all around, use it.

270. Do not try to please everyone, but please yourself.

271. Exercise.

272. Meditate.

273. Walk a mile a day to clear your head.

274. Eat healthy food.

275. Keep your weight in check.

276. Simplify your eating habits.

277. Be enthusiastic about the success of others, your turn will come.

278. Get enough sleep, drink 6 to 8 glasses of water each day.

279 Go for an annual check up.

280. Take care of your teeth. Remember to floss.

281. If someone offers you a breath mint, accept it.

282. Do not chew anything when auditioning.

283. Look clean and neat.

284. Build a simple wardrobe around some primary and medium tone colors.

285. Reduce the clutter in your life.

286. Chiropractic therapy, acupuncture and massage can help relieve tension and stress.

287. Have your eyes checked once a year.

288. Wear clean shoes.

289. Manicure your nails. No dark nail polish.

290. Keep your hair styled and clean.

291. Trim eyebrows and nose hairs.

292. Wax when necessary.

293. Always carry tissues.

294. Shave.

295. Use a good deodorant.

296. Use a body moisturizer if your skin is dry.

297. Participate in sports like swimming, tennis or golf.

298. Be bold with your creativity.

299. Use a sun screen.

300. There is a place for everyone. Go make and take your place.

Note: You do not need to be located in New York, Los Angeles or Chicago to start an acting career. Contact the film commission in your area. Make sure local casting directors and agents are aware of you.

Resource B:

Additional Recommended Resources

Below are lists of materials, readings and resources that we believe you will find helpful as you develop yourself personally and professionally as both actor and human being.

Some of these materials may be purchased from bookstores that cater to the performer such as The Drama Book Shop, Inc., New York or Bakers Plays, Inc., Boston. Others are available from major bookstores around the country and on the internet.

Many libraries include or will include them in their collections if asked. If a specific resource is more easily obtained by ordering directly from its publisher, contact information is provided. Always try to obtain the most current edition of any of the resources listed.

Reference/Business/ Acting/Performing Arts

The following books and programs are of specific interest to actors who wish to learn the business aspects of acting as well as the technique of the art. Some of these books are considered classics, others are viewed as must-reads by *working* actors and industry professionals.

φ Acting World Books – P.O. Box 3899, Hollywood, CA 90078 or (800) 379-5230.

φ Books & Seminars by Lawrence Parke –

Acting Truths and Fictions
The Film Actors Complete Career Guide
How To Start Acting in Film and TV Wherever You Are in America
Since Stanislavski and Vakhtangov (The Method As a System For Today's Actor)
Seminars To Go (Series of 6 books and tapes that cover many aspects of the acting business.)

φ Berland, Terry and Quellette, Deborah - *Breaking Into Commercials*

φ Boyce, Charles - *Shakespeare: A-Z*

φ Chinoy, Helen Krich and Cole, Toby - *Actors on Acting*

φ Eaker, Sherry - *The Back Stage Handbook for Performing Artists, New York Back Stage Books 1995* φ Goldman, William - *The Seasons*

φ Hagen, Uta - *Respect for Acting*

φ Hollywood Reporter - *The Studio Blue-Book*

φ Hook, Ed - *Ultimate Scene and Monologue Source Book*

φ Alterman, Glen – *Promoting Your Acting Career*

φ O'Neil, Brian - *Acting As a Business*

φ See, Joan - *Acting in Commercials*

φ Shurtleff, Micheal - *Audition*

Self Help/Careers/ Motivation/Success

The following are books, books-on-tape, newsletters and programs that *working* actors and industry people have reported as being exceptionally helpful in thinking about their lives, careers and for getting and staying motivated.

φ Ashton Productions Inc. - *Communications to Lighten the Load of Living.* For more information: 1014 Gay St., Sevierville, TN 37862-4213, (888) 222-5170 or API@SSMagnolia.com

φ Bolles, Richard Nelson - *What Color Is Your Parachute?*

φ Hill, Napoleon - *Master Key to Riches*

φ Peale, Norman Vincent - *The Power of Positive Thinking*

φ Peck, M. Scott - *The Road Less Traveled*

φ Phelps, Dr. Susan - *Going All the Way and Making It On the Dirt Road of Life* and *It May Be Good, But Is It Right?* See Ashton Productions, Inc.

φ Sher, Barbara - *I Could Do Anything If I Only Knew What It Was*

φ Shinn, Florence Scovel - *The Game of Life and How to Play It*

φ Schuller, Dr. Robert H. - *If It's Going To Be It's Up To Me*

Resource C:

Quick Summary of Key Casting Guides, Directories and Trades

Below are listed casting guides, directories and trade papers that, as of press time, are updated and published regularly. The guides and directories contain detailed contact information including the names of industry casting personnel that *working* actors stay in touch with on a regular basis.

The trades provide information important to working actors, from audition notices to tracking personnel movements. If any of the guides, directories or trades mentioned are targeted to a specific entertainment market, it is noted.

φ *Academy Players Directory - USA*

φ *Back Stage East/Back Stage West*

φ *Black Talent News - USA*

φ *Breakdown Services - Hollywood Casting Directors Guide*

φ *Chicago Creative Directory*

φ *Henderson's Casting Directors Guide - New York Edition*

φ *Henderson's Personal Managers Directory - USA*

φ *Hollywood Reporter*

φ *Regional Theater Directory - USA*

φ *Ross Reports - New York and Los Angeles*

φ *Show Business*

φ *The Actors Guide - Southeast*

φ *Theatrical Index - USA*

φ *The Hollywood Edition of The Agencies*

φ *The New York Edition of The Agencies*

φ *The Hollywood Acting Coaches and Teachers Directory*

φ *Variety – USA*

Resource D:

Products, Publications and Services of Henderson Enterprises, Inc.

This section contains brief descriptions of the many products, publications and services provided by Henderson Enterprises, Inc., HEI Publications and Sue Porter Henderson. Sample covers of selected publications mentioned earlier in this book are also displayed.

SUE PORTER HENDERSON

is available for personal consultations.

For information and to make an appointment,
Contact her by:

Tel: (212) 472-2292

Fax: (212) 472-5999

Email: sue@hendersonenterprises.com

Or write her at:

Henderson Enterprises
c/o Sue Henderson
360 E. 65th St.
Suite 15E
New York, NY 10021

Henderson Enterprises
Is on the Internet!

Browse our web sites on the web for
our actor services and products.

Visit us at:
http://www.hendersonenterprises.com

Check out our Talent Registry at:
http://www.8x10s.com

For acting related resources, visit:
http://www.actingworld.com

MAILING LABELS

25 Categories from $6 to $19

Our mailing labels are Accurate, Effective, Updated and checked twice monthly. Make sure you send your picture/resume, flyers, postcards, etc., to the RIGHT people at the RIGHT places!

No more wasted or unnecessary duplicates.

Not sure which list you need?

For more information and a
free brochure, contact us by:

Tel: (212) 472-2292

Fax: (212) 472-5999

Email: labels@hendersonenterprises.com

Or place your order on-line on the internet at:

http://www.hendersonenterprises.com

http://www.hendersonenterprises.com

HENDERSON'S
PERSONAL
MANAGERS
DIRECTORY

*Everything You've Always Wanted
To Know About The World Of
Personal Management For
Performing And Other Creative Artists!*

Who They are
How They Build Careers More Swiftly
The Many Things Managers Can Do That Others Can't
How To Seek Them Productively And Successfully

AN HEI PUBLICATION

Henderson's
CASTING DIRECTORS
GUIDE
NEW YORK EDITION
MONTHLY
Compiled For Actors By Working Actors

http://www.hendersonenterprises.com

**Accurate, Effective, Up-Dated & Checked
Monthly, All Casting Directors Including:**

SOAPS
SERIES
AD AGENCIES
PRODUCTION HOUSES
INDEPENDENT CASTING DIRECTORS
that keep files!

AN HEI PUBLICATION

Publications of HEI are available for bulk purchases, educational, business, or sales promotional use. Please direct your inquires or orders to:

Henderson Enterprises
360 E. 65th Street
Suite 15E
New York, NY 10021

Tel: 212-472-2292
Fax: 212-472-5999
E-mail: hei@hendersonenterprises.com
http://www.hendersonenterprises.com